Ivan
the Inventor

Barbara Mitchelhill

Illustrated by
Nick Duffy

OXFORD
UNIVERSITY PRESS

Contents

1 Getting started

My name is Ivan.
Ivan Quiggly.
But they call me
Ivan the Inventor.
Being an inventor is
cool because all the kids
want to know what I'm
up to.

How did I start?
Let me tell you . . .

Getting up every morning was hard for me. I liked to stay in bed and sleep. I had an alarm clock but it never woke me.

I was always late for school and I got into terrible trouble.

I had to think of some way to get to school on time. So I put on my thinking cap and . . . WOW! In seconds, I had a brilliant idea.

I got lots of old things out of the shed. Old clocks, old boots, old springs and wire.

I made a machine to get me up on time every morning.

I'm never going to be late for school again!

The next morning, the machine went off.
Whizz! Bang! Thwack!

I shot out of bed. Cool! My machine had worked and I was up in time for school.

Are you up yet, Ivan?

2 In trouble

My next invention was for my mate, Jazza.
He was just like me – always late. I fixed
springs on his shoes. Brilliant, eh?

Now he could get to school really fast.
He wouldn't be late and he wouldn't get
told off by the Bug. The Bug is our teacher,
Mr Roach. We call him
the Bug because he
has long hairy legs.

But my invention worked too well.
Jazza ran down the street . . .
   BOING! BOING! BOING!

Along the road . . .
   BOING! BOING! BOING!

Across the playground . . .
   BOING! BOING! BOING!
   Then something got in
the way.

It was bad luck that it was the Bug's car.
He went crazy.

"Just look at my car!" he yelled.

"Never mind your car, sir," I said. "Take a look at these springing shoes. Wicked, eh?"

The Bug didn't even look. His face went pale and he began to shake. Just then the bell rang, so Jazza and I ran off.

Just look at my car!

That day went from bad to very bad. Our class had a maths test. I'm no good at maths, but Jazza is worse. We planned our escape.

"Please, sir," I said. "I need the toilet." But the Bug didn't believe me.

Jazza's hand shot up.

"I've got to go and see the Head, sir!" he said. The Bug just shook his head. There was no way out. We had to do it.

That afternoon, the Bug pinned a list on the wall. It was the test results. Jazza's name was at the bottom.

"Jason Brickley," said the Bug, "you can do better. You'll take the test again tomorrow, after school."

Jazza was upset.

As we walked home that day, I put on my thinking cap again. My brain began to buzz.

"Don't worry, Jazza," I said. "I'll help you. I've got an idea."

Jazza looked worried.

3 A new invention

My idea was to make a kind of mobile phone.
It wasn't easy.

After that, we got a book from the library. It told us all we needed to know.

I drew a plan. Then I borrowed some bits from Dad's radio . . . and some from Mum's hairdrier.

This is spaceship Ivan, calling planet Jazza. Can you hear me?

The new mobile was brilliant! My best invention yet. I could talk to Jazza when he was in his bedroom and I was in mine. We had a great time.

I knew my invention would save Jazza. He'd get full marks in the maths test. This is how my plan worked.

Loud and clear, Captain!

After school the next day, Jazza went to the homework room to do the test. He was scared. The Bug put the paper in front of him.

"Do the test and I'll come back in half an hour. Then you can join us on the football pitch."

He left Jazza staring at the test.

While Jazza was doing the test, I went out to the football pitch.

I played for a bit but soon took a dive. I fell over on the grass, holding my leg. I groaned. I moaned. I yelled. The Bug came running to help me.

What happened, Ivan?

It's my leg, sir. Don't worry. I'll just rest it for a bit.

I limped off the pitch and sat behind a tree. The Bug couldn't see me there. I got the mobile out of my sports bag. Then I called Jazza.

Can you hear me, Jazza?

Yes, I can hear you OK.

Brilliant! The plan was going to work.

4 How the plan worked

I got my calculator out of the bag.
"Tell me one of the sums, Jazza," I said.
"126 + 131"

"No problem," I said. I tapped out
the numbers. "257," I said into the
mobile. "Next?"

We had almost finished the test when –
DOOM! – the Bug saw me behind the
tree.

He came over to see what I was up to.
He went crazy when he found out!

I was dragged into school to see the Head. She was mad, too.

"You were cheating!" she said. "That's very bad. And where did you get this thing?"

"I made it," I said.

"You made it?" she said. I don't think she believed me.

"Yes, I did," I said. "Jazza helped, too."

Well, that's amazing, Ivan.

It all turned out OK in the end. Jazza had to do the maths test again, but then we gave a talk to all the kids in the school. It was called "How to make your own mobile phone."

We stood on the stage and told them what to do. Even the teachers were impressed.

Good old Ivan! Good old Jazza!

At the end of the talk the Head gave a speech. "I know that Ivan will never cheat again. But I hope he will invent more things like this mobile phone. It's very clever. Well done, Ivan and Jazza!"

Then she gave us merit badges and everybody cheered.

So you see why they call me Ivan the Inventor. I think up brilliant ideas. This morning the Head came up to me.

"Take a look at this pencil sharpener, will you, Ivan?" she said. "I'm sure you could make something better."

And I will, when I've put on my thinking cap. But don't tell anyone about my cap, will you? That's my secret.